Maine
on my mind

The
Globe
Pequot
Press

Guilford, Connecticut

Library of Congress Number: 90-55078

ISBN 1-56044-029-5

Manufactured in Korea
First Edition/Second Printing

Front cover photos
TOM AKGIRE   *Pemaquid Point Light*
JEFF LEPORE   *Puffin*

Back cover photos
LARRY ULRICH   *Autumn in White Mountain National Forest*
PETER RALSTON   *Boothbay Harbor*
MARK PICARD / N.E. STOCK PHOTO   *Bull moose in Baxter State Park*

Sunrise igniting the harbor at Rockland   MARGO TAUSSIG PINKERTON / N.E.STOCK PHOTO

introduction

I fell in love with Maine at a dangerous age for the American male: forty-five. That was in 1964, when my wife and two children, ages fifteen and thirteen, decided that a small coastal town in Maine was exactly where they wanted to live, not just on vacation but forever. So we came, and it was a deep-sea change from the citified, fast-paced lives we had been living in New York City, Washington, D.C., London, and other foreign cities to which my work had taken me.

I've stayed in love with Maine all twenty-six years since, though the tenor of my love has changed and deepened over the years, as does the love of a man for a woman.

My work is newspapering, and this has allowed me to go almost everywhere in Maine and to meet almost every kind of person. I've talked to Maine fishermen and financiers, Maine governors and truck drivers, Maine lumbermen and legislators. I've done what I wanted to do, gone where I wanted to go, and gotten paid for writing about Maine people and places.

Consequently, during those twenty-six years, more than three million words about Maine have bounced out of my typewriter and into books and newspaper columns. The words are still coming at the rate of about three thousand a week. Almost all are love letters of a kind, celebrating Maine's rugged three-thousand-mile coastline with its inlets, coves, and estuaries;

her mountains, highest east of the Mississippi and long sacred to area Indian tribes; her lovely necklace of islands, where the history of the white man in America began long before the Pilgrims landed at Plymouth Rock; her thousand lakes, where moose, deer, and bears come to drink and where salmon spawn after incredible journeys; and her vast wilderness forests, encompassing more land and more trees than all five other New England states combined. I've also celebrated the good life in Maine's biggest city, Portland, which has only about 61,000 people but more theaters, art galleries, concerts, lawyers, doctors, and restaurants per capita than any other city in the United States. "The finest undiscovered small city in America" is how Portland was described by governors of other states who attended a National Governors Conference here.

The photographs in this handsome book portray many of the astonishing physical beauties of Maine. This visual, physical beauty is enough to make the blood race, to trigger love at first sight. But what is it about Maine that causes that love to grow deeper year after year?

I believe it's the more abstract, even spiritual, qualities that seep slowly, almost imperceptibly into your blood and bone as you live year after year in Maine. The State of Maine—as we like to salute it—becomes a state of mind and attitude, as well as a place. We feel enveloped and possessive, proud and jealous about Maine. It provides an anchor of stability in a too-anchorless, restless world; and we feel blessed for being umbilically linked to its immense and varied landscape-seascape, its history and, above all, its people.

Feelings like this are seldom voiced in Maine. Our Yankee nature is to hide our feelings. But the fact is that almost all the 1.2 million people who live in Maine would rather live here than anywhere else in the world. Millions more from away who've had only vacation tastes of Maine lie awake in city apartments or in suburban houses and dream of the land of their heart's desire—wishing they too could be Mainiacs year-round.

Why is Maine, even the image of Maine, so powerful a magnet to hungering human minds, yearning not only for Maine's beauty and Maine's slower pace, but also for Maine's unwritten but abiding code of values? Lofty generalities, which sounded good when I

Cardinal flower in Mattawamkeag Wilderness Park
GLENN VAN NIMWEGEN

worked in New York City, Washington, and London, don't carry much conviction after twenty-six years of exposure to the practicalities of Maine. So let's get to specifics about how Maine makes this one man feel in his gut as much as in his head. If these specifics have value it is because they are the same kind of gut and mind feelings of millions of others whose lives have been forever spiced by a taste of Maine.

Let me go back to the times when my first infatuation with Maine's beauty began to deepen into a rooted love of the special breed of Maine people.

I'm remembering a snowy night twenty-six years ago. It was our first winter in Damariscotta, Maine, population about one thousand, depending on whether there were births or deaths in the local hospital the night before. My wife and I, still newly transplanted New Yorkers, bundled up and trudged a quarter-mile through snowdrifts to the movies, shown in the old opera house, up a steep flight of stairs, above the grocery store. We bought two tickets for seventy-five cents each from Don Burnham and went into the empty theater and sat and sat, waiting with three other fools who had braved the storm to see a show.

Finally Don Burnham—ticket-seller, candy-seller, and projectionist—came down from his booth to tell us he was cancelling the show because there were only five in the audience. Then Don, whom we barely knew, took my wife and me aside: "Sorry to spoil your night out," he said, refunding our money. "But I've got some good hard cider and some new cards in the kitchen. So the night won't be a bust. Come back and drink a little, play a bit of cards." I had never in my life gone to a movie house like that, where the projectionist suddenly turned into a kitchen-table friend. But that's a slice of Maine.

I'm remembering Merritt Brackett, the boat doctor of New Harbor, the like of whom I've never met anywhere in the world. He was a big man with hands like hams and a slow smile and a slow-talking voice and wire-rimmed spectacles. He was rock-solid and indispensable to the lives and livelihood of half the people in his town. He knew every engine in every boat by its first name. He had installed most of them, so he knew their ailments and foibles from birth. He'd nursed every boat engine through almost every kind of sickness and got it running well again. He was, in short, the family doctor to everything that floated.

If a patient of his took ill at 2 a.m. in a distant port, Merritt would get a phone call. He would throw on his green wool pants, lumberjack shirt, and L.L. Bean boots, lift his huge toolbox into his pickup, and drive through the night. The New Harbor fishermen and their ailing boats were not only Merritt's patients, they were his neighbors and his friends. And that was that. He went whenever, wherever they needed him. And that's a slice of Maine.

Merritt doctored my boat for the twenty years it was moored in New Harbor, prettiest fishing harbor on the Maine coast. We slowly became close friends. Merritt was a breed of man I've found often in Maine, from fishing harbors to north woods. He was quietly but totally competent. He never fretted or panicked at a strange new problem but patiently worked out some way to cope. His feathers wouldn't ruffle, his frustration would never show, even after two or three efforts had failed. He'd just go on and try another way, and another, even if it took all day. His judgment was simple, slow, sensible—on everything from engine parts to the town budget to when the fog would lift. He knew exactly who he was and was happy with the man inside, content with the place where he lived and with the work he did and with the friends he had. Merritt Brackett and his like are the bedrock of Maine. Reliable, reserved, kindly, and so firmly rooted that even a hurricane can't uproot them.

I'm remembering Mabelle, spry, blue-eyed, salty, and staunchly independent until she died two months short of her ninetieth birthday. Mabelle Cotter Alexander Sherman—a big name for a little woman—sold the Sunday

Lesser yellowlegs along the Maine coast GIL LOPEZ-ESPINA

The vibrant colors of a Maine autumn   PETER NESTLER

newspapers from her hole-in-the-wall store on the bridge across the Damariscotta River. She told me, "My father, George Cotter, began selling papers from this store in 1898. I rode on father's horse and wagon to the rail depot to pick up the Sunday papers on the 10:30 train. The Boston Post, the Boston Herald, the Boston Globe and the Boston American. Price was six cents."

Mabelle stands for the continuity, the permanence, the reliability, I believe still exists in Maine more than any other place in the nation. For example, the year Mabelle sold her first Sunday papers, they carried the news that the battleship *Maine* was blown up in Havana harbor, that Admiral Dewey sank the Spanish fleet in Manila Bay, that Teddy Roosevelt led the Rough Riders charging up San Juan Hill. When Mabelle sold her last Sunday paper, it carried the news of President Jimmy Carter's inauguration.

When Mabelle was close to ninety, she slipped on the ice at Christmastime and broke a hip. The day she was to go off to a nursing home, Mabelle decided to die instead. That's being a Mainer right to the last.

Jake Day was my Maine mentor. Few men loved Maine more or knew it better than Jake. He was my neighbor when I first came to Maine, and for some reason he took me under his wing. For eighteen years he taught me the joys of Maine, for which I am forever grateful.

Jake, toward the end of his life, was another of those wonderful, gnarled, strong-rooted Maine men who epitomize the continuity and durability of Maine and her people. Jake, for example, lived in the same house where six generations of Days had lived. He was a painter, a wood carver, a photographer, a storyteller. He went away for a while to work in California, as an artist for Walt Disney. When Disney made his classic film about Bambi the white-tailed deer, it was Jake who made Bambi a white-tailed deer from Maine.

"Look down and walk slowly," Jake told me when he first took me to climb Mount Katahdin, Maine's highest mountain. He showed me tiny ferns, mosses, and flowers that most people would have missed, and he pointed out each find with more delight than if he'd found a nugget of gold. One midnight he put sleeping bags into a canoe and we drifted all night, zippered into our sleeping bags, as he showed me my first Northern Lights. Jake was seventy-four years old that night, but he snorted with pleasure like a young colt in a clover meadow as we watched the Northern Lights race across the sky, leaping from star to star and converging in silent collision at the apex of heaven.

What about the famous, the powerful, the rich in Maine? We have plenty of all these. Yet Mainers make no fuss over them, largely because Mainers don't seem to be impressed much by trappings. They take a man or woman on his or her own merits or faults as a person, a neighbor, another hand held up to vote at Town Meeting or buy a quilt at the church summer sale. The famous in our midst now run from President George Bush, at Kennebunkport, to the Waterville kid of Lebanese extraction, George Mitchell, who is president of the U.S. Senate, to Edmund Muskie, son of a Polish immigrant tailor in the paper-mill town of Rumford who grew up to be Maine's governor, senator, presidential candidate, and the U.S. secretary of state. Most Maine-like of all is that magnificent, enduring woman of Maine, Margaret Chase Smith, now ninety-two, who still goes snowmobiling. She was a telephone operator and a dime-store clerk before she became the most powerful woman in the U.S. Senate. There she showed her plain Maine courage and code of values by becoming the first to denounce Senator Joseph McCarthy from the Senate floor for his outrageous vilification of Americans with whose opinions he clashed.

Moving from politics to the world of letters, E.B. White, this century's purest stylist, wrote most of his books and magazine pieces from his saltwater farm in Brooksville, Maine, where he worked for fifty years. Maine's bestseller these days is Stephen King, of Bangor, who was a teacher in Maine schools before turning to writing horror novels. In painting, we have Andrew and Jamie Wyeth and, before them, Winslow Homer and scores of great American artists of similar stature. Maine may be the only state ever to win five Pulitzer prizes for poetry, fiction, and history within five years.

As for the rich, our island of Mount Desert has been part-time home for generations of the Who's Who of America. Acadia National Park on Mount Desert is the second most visited national park in the nation and the only national park to have been donated to the country, largely by the Rockfeller family, longtime Mount Desert residents.

These are the kinds of Maine people—and there are thousands more—who make Maine such a special place, such a firm and solid anchor to windward in a man's heart.

There are many aspects of love for Maine. Many are linked to the outdoors. Maine seems filled with ardent fishermen, hunters, skiers, mountain climbers, campers, snowmobilers, sailors, canoeists, kayakers, and whitewater rafters. We have our share of hikers, bird-watchers, golfers, tennis players, even polo players. Maine men and women go by the thousands into Maine's vast, unspoiled outdoors. They say it's the sport they're after. But, over a campfire, under the stars, they admit they go to the woods, the lakes, the mountains, and the sea to find serenity, nourishment for the soul, and the comfort of feeling they are an integral, though tiny, part of their eternal universe. Maine people feel that way but never say such words out loud. That's a slice of Maine.

We each have our havens. Mine is the sea, the lonely cove, the uninhabited island. In a thirty-foot, classic wooden cruising boat, I've spent a quarter-century meandering the Maine coast, exploring the islands, gunkholing up rivers and into coves. By midafternoon of a summer cruising day, I've chosen a new island cove in which to set my anchor. I row ashore, explore, swim, dig clams or pick mussels for supper on board. Under the stars, I sit out in the stern, sometimes listening to a great Beethoven symphony blast from my stereo out across the empty ocean; other nights I sit alone in the silent night, listening for the weird cry of a loon, or I lean overboard and drift my fingers through the ocean water, creating a mysterious trail of phosphorescent light in the black velvet night.

Finally clouds obscure the moon. So I go below and sleep, with the ocean lapping at my ear, locked out only by the thickness of a wooden plank. Before first light, I'm back in the stern watching the sun rise up out of the Atlantic, a huge orange globe, a great and wonderful gong heralding a new day coming. And I know that here in a Maine island cove, I'm getting the first kiss, feeling the first warmth, of a new day aborning in America. And I brim with another surge of love for Maine.

Bill Caldwell
Portland, Maine

The town and harbor of Camden GENE AHRENS

> **❝** *To Mainiacs, Maine is not merely a place. It is a spiritual home and shelter as perfectly fitting and comfortable and natural as its shell is to a snail; which, like snails, they carry with them wherever they may go. To them, Maine is a state of mind and a way of life inseparable from the geography and topography of the area and from their own bones and blood and thoughts and dreams. It is an element, as necessary to them as water is to fish. It is almost a religion.* **❞**

Louise Dickinson Rich,
State o' Maine

Dawn at Scarborough Marsh, Maine's largest salt marsh   DOUGLAS MERRIAM

Lobstermen swapping news on the dock at Searsport   DOUGLAS MERRIAM

" *Maine is "small town," and thank God for that. Why? Because in this woebegone welfare world, there is still a human place in small town Maine where people need each other.... **"***

Bill Caldwell,
Enjoying Maine

A peaceful morning in Camden, a popular yachting center nestled beneath the Camden Hills   DAVID MUENCH

Snacktime on Ram Island near Boothbay   PETER RALSTON

13

The town of Vinalhaven, on Vinalhaven Island in Penobscot Bay   DAVID HISER / THE IMAGE BANK

Boatbuilding in Rockport   KIP BRUNDAGE / N.E. STOCK PHOTO

Stephen King—Mainiac and master of horror   DOUGLAS MERRIAM

" *Maine has something—in the character of its plain durable people, in the challenge of its harsh life style, in the raw rugged nature of the land—that draws the artist to it, a catalyst to his creativity.* **"**

Martin Dibner,
Seacoast Maine: People and Places

Day's end at Marshall Point Light at Port Clyde   GALEN ROWELL

British soldier lichen and mountain cranberry on Deer Isle   D. CAVAGNARO

Art imitating life at Nubble Light, York   CRAIG BLOUIN

Red maples living up to their name, Acadia National Park   GLENN VAN NIMWEGEN

A vivid sunset over Rangeley Lake, in the western lake district   RANDY URY / N.E. STOCK PHOTO

" *Bloom-arbored, hundred-harbored,*
Glorious state of Maine,
All the joys of nature
Lie in your domain. "

Mildred Hobbs

Tools of the lobstering trade languishing amid pink cosmos on Monhegan Island PETER RALSTON

Northern red telia sea anemone R. F. LEAHY

Humpback whale in full breach FREDERICK ATWOOD

21

Spires of lupine in Ellsworth   DAVID MUENCH

Double-crested cormorant GIL LOPEZ-ESPINA

> *A flight across America induces the same kind of perspective you get in Maine's north woods, alone in a canoe; or in a small boat anchored in an uninhabited cove on a remote Maine island.*
>
> *This perspective is a sense of being part and parcel of the whole world and all history; a tiny, but integral part of all things; part of the gull flying and the fish swimming and the sun setting and the moon rising and the rock standing, seaweed and mussels clinging to its cold sides, while the wild ocean rolls, everlastingly tugged by the moon and pushed by the wind.*
>
> *In Maine, you seldom voice out loud a thought like this. But you feel it often.*

Bill Caldwell,
Maine Magic

Paddling through the mist on Bryant Pond, near Bethel   JOHN HENDRICKSON

A dory adrift in Stonington Harbor   D. CAVAGNARO

Marsh fern   D. CAVAGNARO

> **"** *What then is the one characteristic that Down East Yankees possess in common, man or woman, Republican or Democrat, Catholic or Protestant, politician, farmer or businessman? It is simply this: every Down-easter knows exactly who he is and feels no compulsion to try to be somebody else.* **"**

Louise Dickinson Rich,
State o' Maine

Setting sail from Green Island, Penobscot Bay   PETER RALSTON

"Bouldering" on Isle au Haut   MICHAEL SACCA / ANIMALS ANIMALS

Spectators at the annual fair in Fryeburg   CRAIG BLOUIN

Commuting to work near North Baldwin, west of Sebago Lake   RANDY URY / N.E. STOCK PHOTO

Boat painter in Stonington
D. CAVAGNARO

Lab worker at salmon hatchery, Eastport
KIP BRUNDAGE / N.E. STOCK PHOTO

❝ *Maine, in spite of her relatively small and scattered population, probably produces a greater crop of individualists than any other state in the Union.* **❞**

Louise Dickinson Rich,
State o' Maine

Retired woodsman, Wells
CRAIG BLOUIN

Lobstering in the morning sun off Cape Porpoise, north of Kennebunkport   CRAIG BLOUIN

Culling out the rejects at Port Clyde, southwest of Thomaston   PETER RALSTON

    " *Lobstermen . . . are in love with their way of life. Nobody tells them what to do; they go out to haul or not as they please, and return when they see fit. They are masters of their environment, handling their boats almost absent-mindedly, with a skill as natural and thoughtless as breathing. They are . . . doing exactly what they want to do most, and doing it well. That's all they ask of life, without even realizing that it is a great deal more than most people get.* **"**

Louise Dickinson Rich,
State o' Maine

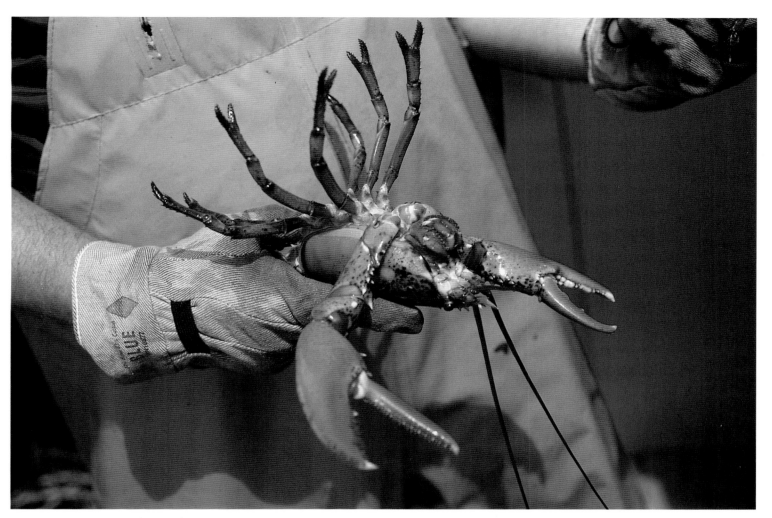

Quality control in Stonington, an unpretentious lobstering town on Deer Isle   D. CAVAGNARO

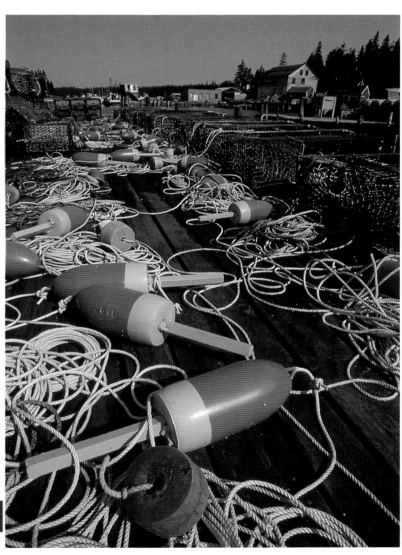

Lobster traps and buoys on the wharf at Port Clyde   RON SANFORD

Belfast lobsterman readying his traps for a day of "setting out"   DOUGLAS MERRIAM

A windjammer catching the breeze in Penobscot Bay   PETER RALSTON

" *I never knew a sensible sailor that wasn't glad to leave the land for the glorious old sea. Their ideas, those land lubbers, about what is comfortable and beautiful, are not worth a ball of spunyarn. They talk to you about the dangers of the sea, just as if there was no lee coast to run one's head and toes against on the land; about the shady groves on a May day, just as if there were no May-day shade under the brave old canvas of Neptune; and about the purling brooks and the music of birds, just as if there were neither water at sea nor any albatross to sail and scream in the sun, nor happy petrels to sing in the storm.* **"**

Thomas Jefferson Farnham,
Travels in the Californias and Scenes
in the Pacific Ocean

Annual wooden boat regatta in Brooklin, home of a nationally known boat-building school   PETER RALSTON

Herring gulls, Acadia National Park   GLENN VAN NIMWEGEN

Repairing the rigging on a schooner docked at Camden   D. CAVAGNARO

Portland Head Light, built in 1791, oldest and one of most scenic lighthouses in Maine   KIP BRUNDAGE / N. E. STOCK PHOTO

> *The coast's symbol of strength and permanence couldn't be a mountain. It has to be a rocky, stormswept headland, with a lighthouse. And it must be both respectful and defiant of the sea. Pemaquid Point, with its famous Pemaquid Light, fulfills these qualifications to the letter.*

Edmund Ware Smith,
A Treasury of the Maine Woods

Pemaquid Point Light guards one of the most rugged stretches of Maine coast

TOM ALGIRE

A fiery Frenchman Bay, east of Bar Harbor   GIL LOPEZ-ESPINA

" *If you like weather, you love Maine. In one day Maine can get up to five kinds of weather. In one year, we get 10 seasons.* "

Bill Caldwell,
Enjoying Maine

A brilliant red maple leaf on a mossy bed   ELEANOR BROWN

Tiger swallowtail among apple blossoms, Deer Isle   D. CAVAGNARO

But perhaps spring fever is not so much an ailment as a moment in time . . . . Perhaps it's when the ice breaks up on the Penobscot River; and when men in the back rooms of Bangor talk about old days on the log drive; and when you suddenly see a foal and its mother lying in the young grass by a white fence; and when you find the blue, broken shell of a small egg and know that a young robin has hatched in a nest invisible in the elm branches waving above you.

Edward Ware Smith,
A Treasury of the Maine Woods

Pussy willows JOHN J. SMITH

Picturesque Rockport, gathering place for artists and musicians   MARGO TAUSSIG PINKERTON / N. E. STOCK PHOTO

Rose hip and rosebud PETER NESTLER

Full speed ahead at the Brooklin wooden boat regatta   PETER RALSTON

" Lovely as summer is, it is a carnival, a time of pleasure and play, of gaudy spinnakers that fill like circus tents, a time of picnics on the rocks, of fast skinny-dipping and moonlight sails. "

Bill Caldwell,
Enjoying Maine

Mountain bikers in Acadia National Park   PETER COLE / N.E. STOCK PHOTO

A rock climber scaling Otter Cliffs on Mount Desert Island   PETER COLE

A Deer Isle meadow carpeted in hawkweed   D. CAVAGNARO

Puffins on Machias Seal Island, one of only two natural nesting sites in the state   VOSCAR / THE MAINE PHOTOGRAPHER

Prelude to winter PETER NESTLER

Bald eagle LYNN M. STONE

> *"When the leaves have turned color, every ridge, every wooded shore line is a joyous picture. The mixture of yellow, orange, red, and dark green is different wherever one looks. . . . Many parts of our country can point to glades or shores or ravines that are as picturesque in Fall. But I have seen no stretch of woods and water where for day after day in the Fall one can travel in solitude and loneliness in corridors as exquisitely decorated as those of the Allagash."*

William O. Douglas,
My Wilderness: East to Katahdin

51

Autumn along the Mattawamkeag River in the Mattawamkeag Wilderness Park   WILLARD CLAY

Scarlet blueberry bushes on Great Head, Mount Desert Island   LARRY ULRICH

Colorful birches and maples along the Wild River in White Mountain National Forest LARRY ULRICH

Snow-covered Mount Katahdin, at 5,267 feet the highest point in Maine   DAVID MUENCH

" *Nowhere does life and the world seem as good as on a bright winter day in Maine. Sit in a snow-cleared spot atop a bold granite boulder, out of the biting north wind. Let the bright winter sun pour down from a pure blue sky and warm you. Let the pure whiteness of untravelled snowfields stretch out before your eyes. . . . Watch a hungry gull arch in the sky and effortlessly ride the currents of air—air that is clear, unpolluted, lovely and icy cold. Drink it till your lungs feel young. Just sit there. And thank God for Maine.* **"**

Bill Caldwell,
Maine Magic

Sledding in South Berwick   CRAIG BLOUIN

Future hockey stars, South Berwick   CRAIG BLOUIN

Dog sledding near Caribou, Aroostook County   DOUGLAS MERRIAM

A wintry day on the harbor at Bernard, Mount Desert Island ART PAINE

The lighthouse on Curtis Island, at the entrance to Camden Harbor in Penobscot Bay   PETER RALSTON

A warm welcome for winter   DOUGLAS MERRIAM

Fogbound in Tenants Harbor, south of Thomaston   PETER RALSTON

" *The firs, the rocks, the lichens, the berries, the birches, and the tamaracks, the seals and gulls that make this meeting of land and water the loveliest I know, all like the fog. When it finally lifted on Thursday, the tourists unzipped their windbreakers and came out blinking into the sun, dazzled by the green shore and blue water. 'Isn't it beautiful?' they said.*

But it wouldn't be, without the fog. "

Charles Kuralt,
Dateline America

A seaman's warning beamed from Petit Manan Island   GIL LOPEZ-ESPINA

Bullfrog   D. CAVAGNARO

“ *On a dark and none too warm evening, the alder swamp rings with the triumphant chorus of a whole nation of spring peepers. The living, exultant noise sounds like a frenzy of tiny sleighbells, and through it one hears the musical trilling of the common toad, and the occasional jug-o-rum of a bull frog. Heard nearby, the din from the swamp is almost deafening. It is a Dionysian ecstasy of night and spring, a shouting and a rejoicing out of puddles and streams, a festival of belief in sheer animal existence.* ”

Henry Beston,
Northern Farm: A Chronicle of Maine

Water lilies on Long Pond below Penobscot Mountain, Mount Desert Island   GLENN VAN NIMWEGEN

Bull moose feeding in Little Kennebago Lake near Rangeley   SCOTT W. SHARKEY

" *Maine's moose, like the giraffe, must be seen to be believed. I have watched a moose step over a six-foot snow fence as though it were a folded lawn chair. Moose are fearless. In the rutting season, a moose will charge a moving car head on. Magnificent to observe, the moose, particularly when he's headed in some other direction.* **"**

Martin Dibner,
Seacoast Maine: People and Places

A birch wood near North Fryeburg, not far from the New Hampshire border   JOHN HENDRICKSON

Trout fishing in the Androscoggin River in western Maine   APPEL COLOR PHOTOGRAPHY

" *There are the rivers—the Kennebec, the Androscoggin, the Penobscot and the wild Allagash—tumbling from the hills, sweeping across the lowlands, hurrying to keep their appointments with the sea. They are not the longest rivers in the world, nor the oldest, nor the most important, but they may very well be the best loved. They're of a convenient size to be taken to the heart.* **"**

Louise Dickinson Rich,
State o' Maine

Bull moose, the state animal, in Baxter State Park   ALAN D. BRIERE

White-tailed doe and twins   MARK F. WALLNER

Kayaking on the West Branch of the Penobscot River, one of the most spectacular whitewater rivers in the East   ART PAINE

The endangered peregrine falcon   MARK PICARD / N.E. STOCK PHOTO

At the summit of Mount Katahdin, centerpiece of Baxter State Park   CRAIG BLOUIN

" Man is Born to Die, His Works are Short-lived
Buildings Crumble, Monuments Decay, Wealth Vanishes
But Katahdin in All its Glory
Forever Shall Remain the Mountain of the
People of Maine. "

Percival P. Baxter,
founder of Baxter State Park

Boulder-strewn Taylor Pond, below Mount Katahdin   DAVID MUENCH

> **"** *These open woods are also the place for man. Visibility may never be more than fifty yards. Every glade is a study in distinction. One who walks it moves quietly and discreetly, out of hope, not fear. The hope is the rich reward of a grouse going out underfoot, a bear feeding, or a deer, frozen, with ears up, eyes glistening and white tail switching. Or the reward may be a porcupine or, less likely, a raccoon, or only the flash of a northern flicker. The wonders of Maine are ceaseless. Every trip into these open woods is adventure, bringing the excitement of discovery.* **"**

William O. Douglas,
My Wilderness: East to Katahdin

Cedar waxwing   ALAN D. BRIERE

Raccoon   PETER NESTLER

Springtime along Jesup Path, in Acadia National Park   GLENN VAN NIMWEGEN

Cascading falls on 1,530-foot Cadillac Mountain, Mount Desert Island   GLENN VAN NIMWEGEN

Wood lily CRAIG BLOUIN

Maple leaves, mushrooms, and coral fungus near Fryeburg JOHN HENDRICKSON

" *The black branches and gleaming white trunks of the paper birch never make a neat, symmetrical picture. The trees lean this way and that at crazy angles, as if some impressionistic painter has arranged the scene. . . . They were at their best on wet, gloomy days, when rain dripped from the leaves. Then they lighted the whole forest and made it gleam. They brought brightness on dark days, and made the heart rejoice.* "

William O. Douglas,
My Wilderness: East to Katahdin

Autumn mist among the birches near Stow, north of Fryeburg JOHN HENDRICKSON

A farmer training his oxen to the yoke in Acton, northwest of Sanford   CRAIG BLOUIN

" To Maniacs, the world is divided into Maine and elsewhere. "

Louise Dickinson Rich,
State o' Maine

Keeper of the Nubble Light, York   CRAIG BLOUIN

A Stonington lobsterman finishing a cold day's work   JEFF DWORSKY

A Stonington fisherman repairing his net   D. CAVAGNARO

Digging for clams near Cushing, southwest of Thomaston   PETER RALSTON

Coiled and at the ready   MARY ELLEN SCHULTZ

“ *I call them fishermen, but the term and the rubber boots loosely includes the run of our people who live by the sea. There are true fishermen among them with their own boats, there are clammers whom the state authorities are forever checking; there are lobstermen with their boats and lobster traps, there are diggers of the seaworms which are used for bait;... Whatever they may chance to be, and whether boat owners or clammers, one great influence binds them all together; they are people of the sea.* ”

Henry Beston,
Northern Farm: A Chronicle of Maine

NIGHTOWL

Unloading herring at Carvers Harbor on Vinalhaven Island   RANDY URY / N.E. STOCK PHOTO

Full moon over the Breakwater Light on Rockland Harbor   PETER RALSTON

Moving sheep from island to island in Muscongus Bay   PETER RALSTON

Pemaquid Point Light, one of more than seventy lighthouses in Maine   RON SANFORD.

Sunrise over Quoddy Head, easternmost point in the United States   WILLARD CLAY

❝ *But the first salt wind from the east, the first sight of the lighthouse set boldly on its outer rock, the flash of a gull, the waiting procession of seaward-bound firs on an island, made me feel solid and definite again, instead of a poor, incoherent being. Life was resumed, and anxious living blew away as if it had not been. I could not breathe deep enough or long enough. It was a return to happiness.* **❞**

Sarah Orne Jewett,
The Country of the Pointed Firs
and Other Stories

Otter Cliffs and Newport Cove, Mount Desert Island   LARRY ULRICH

Day dawning at Ogunquit, an Indian name meaning "beautiful place by the sea"   CRAIG BLOUIN

" *Its voice is always in the ear, sometimes subdued and wooing, sometimes as murmurous as the slow breathing of a sleeping beast, sometimes as wild and clamorous as a battle cry. All other sounds—the calling of birds, the wind over the heath, the speech of men—are flute notes against the deep orchestration of the sea.* **"**

Louise Dickinson Rich,
The Peninsula

Harbor seals hauling out at Bar Harbor   FRED ATWOOD

Northern red telia sea anemone   R. F. LEAHY

Wolffish amid anemones   R. F. LEAHY

Gorham Mountain and The Beehive guarding the rocky shoreline of Acadia National Park   GLENN VAN NIMWEGEN

" *The power of the surf. . . is manifest in a slow-motion action that gives no indication at first of the energy involved. No shallow water borders this exposed side so the waves do not break before striking the cliffs. Instead, they draw back and rise against them slowly, noiselessly, as though they would gently lap the face of the rock. Suddenly, just before the wave peak reaches the cliffs, something happens to the calm coherence of the wave. It spreads into a massive sheet of blue-green water that climbs up the face of the rock, disintegrates, and widens into a fan of white spray and foam that crashes down on land and sea.* **"**

Eliot Porter,
Summer Island

Sea spray on Schoodic Point, Acadia National Park   GIL LOPEZ-ESPINA

Lone lobsterman hauling traps off Mount Desert Island   PETER RALSTON

A beachcomber's bonanza, Deer Isle   D. CAVAGNARO

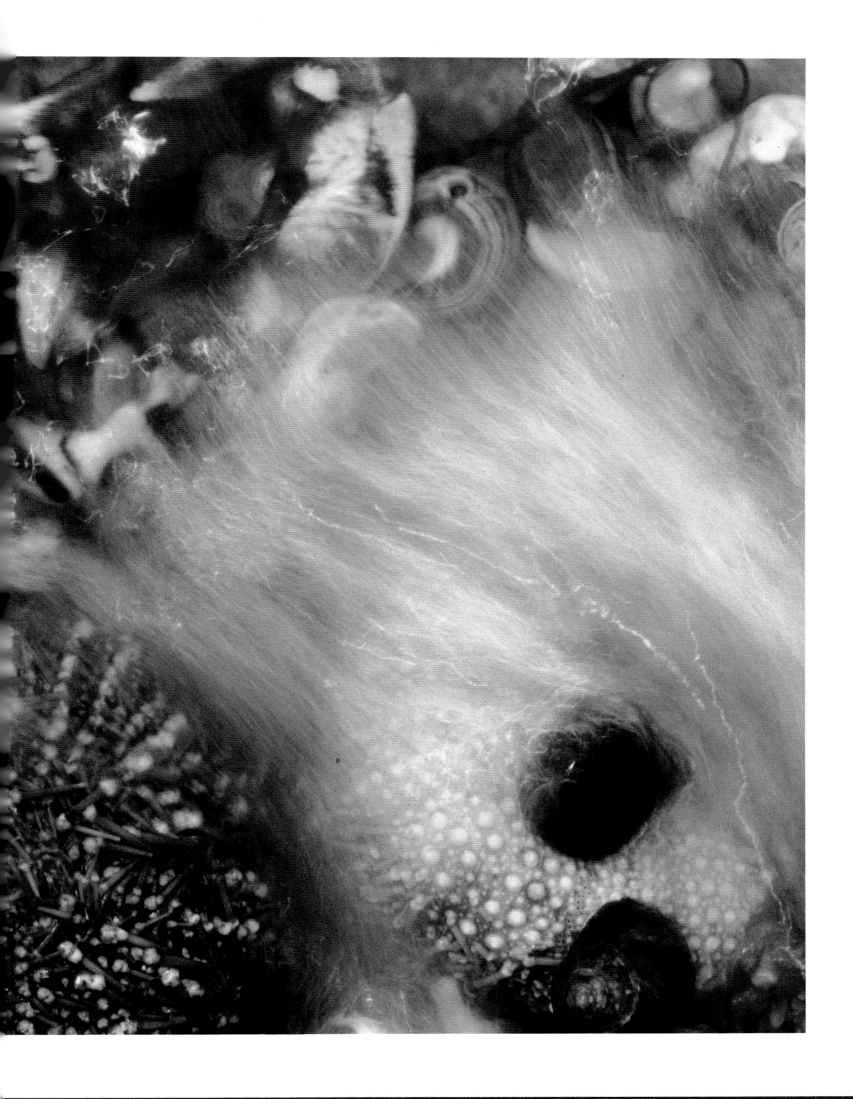

Pitcher plants, laurel, and mosses on Great Wass Island, a Nature Conservancy preserve   DAVID MUENCH

Black-capped chickadee, the state bird RANDY URY / N.E. STOCK PHOTO

> *It is a country full of evergreen trees, of mossy silver birches and watery maples, the ground dotted with insipid, small red berries and strewn with damp and moss-grown rocks—a country diversified with innumerable lakes and rapid streams. . .the forest resounding at rare intervals with the note of the chickadee, the blue jay and the woodpecker, the scream of the fish hawk and the eagle, the laugh of the loon and the whistle of ducks along the solitary streams.*

Henry David Thoreau,
The Maine Woods

Chipmunk dining on blueberries, Baxter State Park ALAN D. BRIERE

> **"** *The green meadows were covered with the geese, white, close-set, like foam caught in the grasses when a tide goes out, or perhaps like banks of snow beginning to soften in the spring. Above them flew other flocks of geese, perhaps a dozen or a hundred or five hundred together, some flying low, some high up in the air, circling over the meadows or the blue river, flying slowly against the cold wind, or swiftly with it. In spite of black wing-tips, they were apparently pure white as the sun struck them, and dark as they turned, each group and wheeling squadron continually honking as it flew, continually answered by the multitude below, in one wild lovely monotonous clangor like nothing we have ever heard.* . . . **"**

Elizabeth Coatsworth,
Maine Memories

A blizzard of migrating snow geese   JEFF LEPORE

The granite summit of Cadillac Mountain overlooking Otter Point on Mount Desert Island   LARRY ULRICH

" *All I could see from where I stood*
Was three long mountains and a wood;
I turned and looked the other way,
And saw three islands in a bay. "

Edna St. Vincent Millay,
Collected Poems

Northern pitcher plants cradling raindrops   PETER NESTLER

> **"** *Keep who will the city's alleys,*
> *Take the smooth-shorn plain—*
> *Give to us the cedar valleys,*
> *Rocks and hills of Maine!* **"**

John Greenleaf Whittier,
The Lumbermen

Night lights of Portland, largest city in Maine   RANDY URY / N.E. STOCK PHOTO

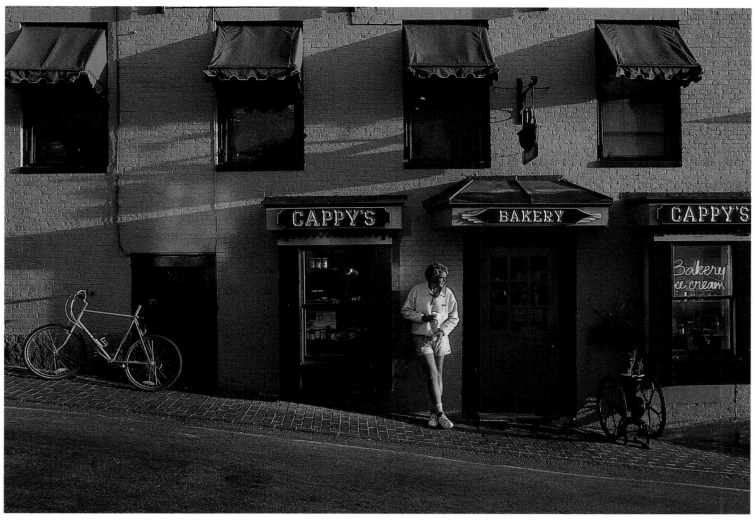

Sunday morning coffee in Camden   DOUGLAS MERRIAM

Sun catchers at a shop in Boothbay   G. SCHUYLER

Boating on Eagle Lake, Acadia National Park   GLENN VAN NIMWEGEN

" *I like to think of the lakes coming down from the north of us like a gigantic staircase to the sea. Kennebago to Rangeley to Cupsuptic, down they drop, level to level, through short, snarling rivers; Mooselukmeguntic to the Richardsons to Pond-in-the-River, and through Rapid River to Umbagog, whence they empty into the Androscoggin and begin the long south-easterly curve back to the ocean.* "

Louise Dickinson Rich,
We Took to the Woods

Male wood ducks LARRY R. DITTO

Kayaker contemplating Togue Pond, just outside Baxter State Park DOUGLAS MERRIAM

The Bubble Mountains reflected in Eagle Lake DAVID MUENCH

Overlooking Moosehead Lake, largest of the state's six thousand lakes and ponds   DOUGLAS MERRIAM

Great blue heron   RANDY URY / N.E. STOCK PHOTO

The quintessential Maine meal D. CAVAGNARO

A blueberry harvest near Union RON SANFORD

> *Maine foods in their seasons flash across your palate. The first clams dug after ice is out. Spring and the first trout. The first fiddleheads. Salmon. Lobsters, when the price drops. Then shedders in July boiled up on an island shore. Berries—blackberries, blueberries, raspberries picked wild and all eaten till your face and hands are colored, your shirt stained and your tummy full. Venison steaks. Fresh fish chowder with big chunks of haddock and hake. Native corn roasted in the husk. MacIntosh apples in the Fall. Cider pressed fresh at a friend's farm. Sauerkraut made the Waldoboro way.*

Bill Caldwell,
Enjoying Maine

Picking apples in Searsmont DOUGLAS MERRIAM

Maple sugaring near Rumford BUDD TITLOW

Collecting clams TED LEVIN

Potato fields stretch to the horizon in Aroostook County, Maine's vast northern crown   DOUGLAS MERRIAM

Excused from school to pick potatoes   DOUGLAS MERRIAM

A gentle sunset over a portion of "The County"   DOUGLAS MERRIAM

❝ *. . . the land goes on and on and on—no fences, hardly any hills, scarcely any trees. Just fields so big they seem to have no end. The only interruptions are a few white farmhouses every mile or so, standing there alone, unpretentious, unsoftened by trees and gardens.* **❞**

Bill Caldwell,
Enjoying Maine

Lush farmland near Cornish, west of Sebago Lake   CRAIG BLOUIN

Fresh vegetables for sale at North Berwick   CRAIG BLOUIN

Broccoli flourishing on a Presque Isle farm DOUGLAS MERRIAM

Bunchberry leaves catching the rain, Acadia National Park   GLENN VAN NIMWEGEN

> " *A rainy day is the perfect time for a walk in the woods. . .always thought so myself; the Maine woods never seem so fresh and alive as in wet weather. Then, all the needles on the evergreens wear a sheath of silver.* "

Rachel Carson,
The Sense of Wonder

Big Heath, a 420-acre peatland in Acadia National Park   DAVID MUENCH

A covered bridge over the Sunday River, near Newry   JEFF GNASS

Paper birches along a tributary of the Bear River in Grafton Notch State Park PETER COLE

" Mainiacs away from Maine are truly displaced persons, only half alive, only half aware of their immediate surroundings. Their inner attention is always preoccupied and pre-empted by the tiny pinpoint on the face of the globe called Down East. They try to live not in such a manner that they will eventually be welcomed into Paradise, but only so that someday they can go home to Maine. "

Louise Dickinson Rich,
State o' Maine

A dramatic sunrise over Ocean Park   EMERY SANTERRE

The schooners *Heritage* and *American Eagle* at dock in Rockland   MARGO TAUSSIG PINKERTON / N.E. STOCK PHOTO

Lobster pot buoys on a wall in Newagen, on Sheepscot Bay   TOM ALGIRE

they made it possible

Maine on my Mind would have been impossible to produce without the creative and technical skills of more than fifty professional photographers. These men and women succeeded in a difficult task—capturing the many moods and faces of the Pine Tree State.

From majestic seascapes to delicate lilies, Maine contains a breathtaking array of beautiful images, but transforming these images onto film requires more than just a camera. It takes an eye for composition, technical expertise, long hours of work, and the sheer determination to obtain a memorable shot rather than a mere snapshot.

The photographers for *Maine on my Mind* provided this extra skill and effort. They sailed, hiked, climbed, waited, and watched to get the best possible images from all parts of the state.

To all the excellent photographers who contributed to *Maine on my Mind*, thank you.

The Globe Pequot Press

Photographers in *Maine on my Mind*

Tom Algire	Gil Lopez-Espina	Mark Picard	Budd Titlow
Appel Color Photography	Jeff Gnass	Margo Taussig Pinkerton	Larry Ulrich
Frederick D. Atwood	John Hendrickson	Peter Ralston	Randy Ury
Craig Blouin	David Hiser	Galen Rowell	Voscar/The Maine Photographer
Alan D. Briere	R.F. Leahy	Michael Sacca	Mark F. Wallner
Eleanor Brown	Jeff Lepore	Ron Sanford	And these photo agencies:
Kip Brundage	Ted Levin	Emery Santerre	Animals Animals
D. Cavagnaro	Douglas Merriam	Mary Ellen Schultz	Naturegraphs
Willard Clay	David Muench	G.L. Schuyler	New England Stock Photo
Peter Cole	Peter Nestler	Scott W. Sharkey	The Image Bank
Larry R. Ditto	Glenn Van Nimwegen	John J. Smith	
Jeff Dworsky	Art Paine	Lynn M. Stone	

Last shot of the day on Pemaquid Point   GALEN ROWELL

acknowledgments

The publishers gratefully acknowledge the following sources:

Pages 8, 26, 28, 30, 64, 76 and 114 from *State o' Maine* by Louise Dickinson Rich. Copyright © 1964 by the author. Published by Harper & Row, Publishers, Inc.

Pages 10, 40, 46, 104 and 107 from *Enjoying Maine* by Bill Caldwell. Copyright © 1977 by the author and Guy Gannett Publishing Co.

Pages 14 and 62 from *Seacoast Maine: People and Places* by Martin Dibner. Copyright © 1973 and 1987 by the author and George A. Tice. Published by The Harpswell Press.

Pages 22 and 54 from *Maine Magic* by Bill Caldwell. Copyright © 1979 by the author and Guy Gannett Publishing Co.

Pages 38 and 42 from *A Treasury of the Maine Woods* by Edmund Ware Smith. Copyright © 1958 by the author. Published by Fredrick Fell, Inc., Publishers.

Pages 50, 70 and 74 from *My Wilderness: East to Katahdin* by William O. Douglas. Copyright © 1961 by the author. Published by Pyramid Publications, Inc.

Page 58 from *Dateline America* by Charles Kuralt. Copyright © 1979 by CBS Inc. Published by Harcourt, Brace & Jovanovich.

Pages 60 and 80 from *Northern Farm: A Chronicle of Maine* by Henry Beston. Copyright © 1948 by the author. Published by Ballantine Books, Inc.

Page 84 from *The Country of the Pointed Firs and Other Stories* by Sarah Orne Jewett. Copyright © 1896 by the author. Published by Houghton Mifflin Co.

Page 86 from *The Peninsula* by Louise Dickinson Rich. Copyright © 1958 by the author. Published by J.B. Lippincott Co.

Page 88 from *Summer Island* by Eliot Porter. Copyright © 1968 by the Sierra Club and Ballantine Books.

Page 93 from *The Maine Woods* by Henry David Thoreau. Published 1864 by Ticknor and Fields.

Page 94 from *Maine Memories* by Elizabeth Coatsworth. Copyright © 1968 by the author. Published by The Stephen Greene Press.

Page 96 from *Collected Poems* by Edna St. Vincent Millay. Published 1967 by Harper & Row, Publishers, Inc.

Page 97 from *The Complete Poetical Works of John Greenleaf Whittier*. Published 1883 by Houghton, Mifflin and Co.

Page 100 from *We Took to the Woods* by Louise Dickinson Rich. Copyright © 1942 by the author. Published by J.B. Lippincott Co.

Page 110 from *The Sense of Wonder* by Rachel Carson. Copyright © 1956 by the author. Published by Harper & Row, Publishers, Inc.

About Bill Caldwell

A longtime newspaperman, Bill Caldwell believes, "Maine is the best beat of all." His columns about Maine appear in the *Portland Press Herald* and the *Maine Sunday Telegram*. Before he joined Gannett newspapers in Maine, he spent seven years in Washington under President Eisenhower as Assistant Director of Foreign Operations, flew bombers in World War II, and went to Cambridge University and the Sorbonne in Europe. He is the author of ten books, including *Enjoying Maine, Maine Magic, Islands of Maine, Rivers of Fortune, Lighthouses of Maine,* and *The Maine Coast.* He lives in Portland.

Sandy Popham Beach, in Popham Beach State Park south of Bath LARRY ULRICH